MYIA

I AM
More

365 EMPOWERING DAILY AFFIRMATIONS
for Teens and Young Adults

outskirts
press

Outskirts Press, Inc.
http://www.outskirtspress.com

ISBN: 978-1-4787-8788-4

PRINTED IN THE UNITED STATES OF AMERICA

Acknowledgements

I give all thanks and honor to God. A very special thank you to my 17-year-old niece, Bre'Auria Wherry, for helping me to ensure this book was teen friendly as well as her encouragement, love and support along the way. To all of my nieces and nephews, I am more because of you and every student that I've had the honor to teach, counsel, coach, and mentor. Finally, every teen and young adult who opens this book, I am proud of you for aspiring to be better persons. Be Empowered!

Table of Contents

Day 1

I am plentiful; helpful in many ways. There are great gifts on the inside of me—enough to share my presence through deeds and words with the world. I am valuable and appreciated. I AM MORE abundant.

Day 2

I am a bright figure everywhere I go, even in the still moments. My personality lights up the room and my huge heart lifts others up. My smile gives life. I AM MORE animated.

Day 3

I stand up for myself. I respect all of God's creation; therefore, I am respected. I have infinite gifts, talents and passion to offer. I am confident in my decisions. I AM MORE assertive.

Day 4

A lot of people look up to me, even when I'm not noticing my impact. I am a leader that influences others to do and be great whether people are looking or not. Treating my counterparts how I would like to be treated is my motto. I AM MORE admirable.

Day 5

I am a beautiful/handsome person inside and out, like an eagle who is amazing to watch while soaring, but even better noticed when spreading its wings. I am strong and resilient. I lift people up so we can all fly high together. I AM MORE attractive.

Day 6

I am an activist. I think and then speak my mind about what is right and what is wrong. I help others see the good in challenging situations. I AM MORE brave.

Day 7

I think fast, especially in tight and risky situations. I stay on my feet to keep on top of my game. I do my best to make great decisions; they teach me the difference between what's good and what's not so good, and it's worth it. I AM MORE witty.

Day 8

I am observant. With all my senses, I tune in to life. I see things for what they are without assumptions. I listen to verbal and non-verbal communication. I AM MORE objective.

Day 9

I do my best to be there for others when they are in times of need. Keeping my word is very important to me and the people, places and things that I commit to; moreover, making a difference in the lives of others matters most to me. I AM MORE available.

Day 10

I am a winner; I am determined to meet every goal I set. Motivation is how I thrive and completing what I start is my primary focus. I AM MORE accomplished.

Day 11

I am adored by a great number of people. Large numbers of talented individuals follow my lead because I inspire them to do the right thing. I AM MORE valuable.

Day 12

I am knowledgeable, needing to know more information in-depth. I ask many questions not caring what others think, so I can make the best decisions. I am edgy in my thinking and creative process; I like being in the know. I AM MORE curious.

Day 13

Having the courage to help others has caused me to become a shining star. My actions inspire people in a positive way. My inner glow reflects the goodness of my heart's intent. I beam joy and life. I AM MORE radiant.

Day 14

I am well-mannered and well kept. I am healthy in mind, body and soul. I am self-respected, well dressed and always present myself with style. I AM MORE classic.

Day 15

I am full of life—never overworked. I am happy and enthusiastic. I AM MORE energized.

Day 16

Smoking is not my thing; alcohol cramps my style, and abstinence is my plan until marriage. I am a dignified person who is above the influence and above destroying my body. I AM MORE pure.

Day 17

I keep my hair well groomed. I am responsible for myself. My self-esteem is very high because I encourage myself. My worth is not dictated by the opinions of others, but more importantly, who I know myself to be in the absence of those opinions. What I believe about myself is of the highest value. I AM MORE worthy.

Day 18

I am peaceful. I do not believe in using violence as a way to manipulate others into doing something that I want them to do. I keep my composure when the feeling of anger arises. I AM MORE calm.

Day 19

I do my best to have good intentions as well as actions. I will pay more attention to other people's feelings, including my own. I AM MORE caring.

Day 20

When I am emotional, no matter whether happy or sad, I will freely acknowledge my feelings and openly be honest with myself and others, regarding my truest self-expressions. I will do my best to maintain a positive outlook even when I am challenged. I AM MORE authentic.

Day 21

I love to laugh even without reason. I am generous, excited and enthusiastic about life. I brighten people's days. I AM MORE bubbly.

Day 22

Others can trust me. I do not bite the hand of those who are good to me and do not gossip about my closest friends. I AM MORE loyal.

Day 23

I enjoy being young yet with a level of maturity all at the same time. I love having fun. Little things make me happy. I do my best not to worry too much because I AM MORE youthful.

Day 24

The truth is the way to go because lies will get me into trouble. I feel light and free from guilt when I do the right thing. I stand for the truth. I AM MORE honest.

Day 25

I don't take people for granted. I am appreciative. I have gratitude. I am thankful for what I have. I AM MORE humble.

Day 26

I don't always follow the crowd and that's a great thing. I am my own person. I am unique with my own sauce. I AM MORE of an individual.

Day 27

I am brilliant. I am awesome; however, I am un-afraid to ask for assistance. I notice important actions on behalf of community leaders. I am smart yet humble. I put myself in the right situations and around the right people. I AM MORE resourceful.

Day 28

There is only one of me. I am worth a lot. No one can replace me. There cannot be another me. I am a good person with goals, good intentions and a future. I am priceless.

Day 29

I keep my word. I will not back out unless I first communicate with whomever I've made a commitment to. I honor others as well as their time. I have more character.

Day 30

Everyone is different, whether it is personality or appearance. I do not judge anyone. I don't know what most people are going through, therefore, I don't put myself above others. I AM MORE accepting.

Day 31

I strive to be happy. I stay on my grind, never giving up. I love to be successful. I feed myself positive thoughts every day. I will not fail because I AM MORE motivated.

Day 32

I follow the rules that are given to me. I do my best to do good so that I can follow the footsteps of great leaders. I am becoming a better person each day, always striving to reach my highest spiritual potential. I look to my Creator for guidance. I AM MORE divine.

Day 33

I don't always speak my mind. I sometimes keep my progress and success to myself. I'm not sneaky, but I move in silence. I AM MORE discreet.

Day 34

I am lively in attitude. I am always on my toes and very upbeat. I AM MORE vivacious.

Day 35

I am family-oriented and I love being surrounded by their individual presence. I am not isolated from the people I love, because I know that they love me too. I get excited about spending time with the people that are on my side. I AM MORE present with loved ones.

Day 36

I eat right to stay in shape. I am positive-minded and I believe in being balanced. I like to enjoy life. I AM MORE healthy.

Day 37

I encourage others to do well. I push myself to do better. I am here to share what's right. I do my best to be by the side of others in times of need and also when they have more than enough. I AM MORE supportive.

Day 38

I am calm, not rowdy. I am cool. I let my mind flow free. I am relaxed with no real drama. I AM MORE peaceful.

Day 39

I have no static; life is flowing for me. I am in rhythm; things just seem to be going my way. My days are great. I wake up with a smile on my face. I AM MORE serene.

Day 40

I do my best in school and try my hardest at everything I do in order to succeed. My success shows through all my efforts. I AM MORE rewarded.

Day 41

My ability to go above and beyond causes me to stand out. Others notice me due to my accomplishments and optimistic attitude. I AM MORE recognized.

Day 42

My style is different. I think for myself. I cannot be compared to others or even put in the same category, because I AM MORE unique.

Day 43

I am here to keep an eye on people younger than myself. I am here to guide them in the right direction. I AM MORE of a mentor.

Day 44

I am not the type to draw attention to myself. I am noticed more when I listen. My silent ways cause others to wonder. I AM MORE mysterious.

Day 45

I am a work in progress. I have multiple strengths as well as weaknesses. Loving myself helps me to accept both aspects of who I am. I AM MORE conscious.

Day 46

I do not bottle up my emotions. I am sometimes outspoken. Communication is very important in all my relationships. I AM MORE expressive.

Day 47

I am unpredictable, which sometimes makes life exciting. When I show up, others react in 'awe.' Miracles happen in my life daily. I AM MORE sensational.

Day 48

I am well put together—no blemishes. I am a lady/ gentleman. I hold my head up when I walk. I am classic. I AM MORE polished.

Day 49

I have a voice. I have authority. I am connected to others. My mind is sharp. I AM MORE powerful.

Day 50

There is no need for makeup or excessive lengths of unnatural hair. There is no need for a false personality and obsessive tattoos. I AM MORE natural.

Day 51

I am a child of my God. He is my Father. I believe in Him. He is holy, powerful and the Almighty One. I speak to Him when I am alone. I AM MORE spiritual.

Day 52

I take action when something is not right. I stand up for my rights. I AM MORE liberal.

Day 53

I live in my own world. I create pictures and paintings of dreams, goals and visions that I want to achieve. I am free; free to be whatever I desire. I AM MORE imaginative.

Day 54

Music sends my mind on a journey. It sometimes helps me to connect emotionally to my present situations. Songs are therapeutic for my soul. I feel like I am in a world of my own when I hear certain beats. Music gives me a break from the world. I AM MORE musical.

Day 55

I am one: one with God, one with peace, one with belief, one with great judgment. I AM MORE in tune.

Day 56

I am a princess/prince in the making, becoming a queen/king. I am put up on a pedestal. I am infused with power. I AM MORE royal.

Day 57

I will be remembered for my accomplishments. I may not be a 'Michael' or 'Whitney'; however, I will be remembered through my own inspirational influences, gifts and talents that I share with people. I AM MORE legendary.

Day 58

I am unforgettable. I am above average. I am unique. Many people adore my presence. I AM MORE impressionable.

Day 59

All eyes are on me. I may not try to draw attention, but I do. I am a different breed. I am not like others. I am extravagant; the center of attention. I AM MORE well-regarded.

Day 60

My eyes tell stories; my walk exudes confidence. I have depth. My presence is seen in 3-D. I AM MORE magnificent.

Day 61

I am not able to be copied. There isn't another person made like me. My genius is authentically abundant. I AM MORE original.

Day 62

I have my own voice. No one can stop my dreams. I have my own mind. I make my own choices. I AM MORE free.

Day 63

I am kind. I am friendly. I am optimistic. I AM MORE generous.

Day 64

I am my own person, inspired by some. I look up to a few, but I am a uniquely creative individual. I make my own decisions and enjoy my freedom to choose my attitude on life. I AM MORE responsible.

Day 65

I am the warm hug that everyone needs. I am the smile that brightens people's days. I am the advice that people look for. I am the care that many need. I AM MORE loving.

Day 66

I laugh. I make people laugh. I am funny. I help others enjoy their time in my presence. I AM MORE comical.

Day 67

I handle my own business. I am responsible and trustworthy. I don't need too much from others. I AM MORE independent.

Day 68

I stand my ground. I am confident but not arrogant or conceited. I am content with a little or a lot. Simplicity is my driving force. I AM MORE modest.

Day 69

We are all human beings with different intentions. No one is better than another. We are equal. I am level in my thinking of others. I AM MORE easygoing.

Day 70

I have obstacles each day, however, it is my resilience that gets me over each hurdle. I don't cry or complain about them. I AM MORE solid.

Day 71

I should be treated like royalty, not disrespected. I should be given all the attention and affection I need. I AM MORE deserving.

Day 72

I am sensitive and fragile sometimes. It's ok for me to be open and vulnerable about my feelings. I AM MORE precious.

Day 73

I am here for everyone. I support others. Feeding the homeless and giving clothes to the shelter make life easier for everyone. I AM MORE giving.

Day 74

Everything about me was created perfectly. My imperfections are what make me perfect according to my Creator. I AM MORE special.

Day 75

I am refreshing. I am "the break from the world" that people dream about. I am like a glass of the most thirst-quenching water for the parched. I AM MORE delightful.

Day 76

I am here to listen. I will stay quiet and keep a secret. My closest friends are welcome to vent to me. I am your diary. I AM MORE friendly.

Day 77

I will keep everything positive and will still tell the truth, no matter how much it hurts. I will share what's right. I AM MORE genuine.

Day 78

I may not have everything I want, but I have everything I need: love, happiness and a great personality. I AM MORE complete.

Day 79

Even with insecurities, I still appreciate myself because I know my worth. I speak positive words over myself and regard others with the same respect. I like who I am and what I offer to the world. I AM MORE cherished.

Day 80

I am trusting. No one is guilty until proven guilty. I would like people to trust me, so I AM MORE trusting. I give people the benefit of the doubt. I AM MORE trustworthy.

Day 81

I am clear with my intentions. I enjoy allowing others to make their own decisions when it comes to me. I use discretion when first meeting new people. "Drama-free" is my motto. I am comfortable with keeping to myself sometimes. I AM MORE private.

Day 82

My excitement pulls people into my space. My actions influence others to be more liberated. I AM MORE electrifying.

Day 83

I am determined to be a force to be reckoned with in this world. I will be steadily keeping my eyes on the prize and no one can stop me but me. I AM MORE focused.

Day 84

I am kindhearted. I give people multiple chances, but I am not a pushover. I AM MORE forgiving.

Day 85

I am the one: the one that will shine, shine bright; the one that will make it in life; the one everyone will know. I AM MORE exceptional.

Day 86

I am a painting. Someone created me. I am full of meaning. I am something like Jackson Pollack, abstract. I AM MORE artistic

Day 87

I am polished. I make sure I speak with manners and proper grammar. I am educated. I AM MORE knowledgeable.

Day 88

Others benefit from me because I have a lot to offer. The people that are around me are influenced by me. I AM MORE beneficial.

Day 89

Everyone loves me. I allow people to fall fast for me. My words are smooth and actions are suave. I AM MORE charming.

Day 90

I rub off on people. Whatever I do, others follow. I have a swift way of doing things. I am the alpha. I AM MORE influential.

Day 91

I am a communicator. I communicate very well. My body language is respectful. I use eye contact when talking to others. Non-verbal communication is just as important as verbal communication. I AM MORE articulate.

Day 92

My work is always finished on time. I am not distracted. I am hard working and focused. I AM MORE accomplished.

Day 93

I love the positive influence of money. I earn money to live as well as to give. Money is not my world but it is a necessity. It is my responsibility to build capital to invest in my dreams, goals and aspirations. Money is not happiness, but the resources it provides helps to make people, places, things and me richer. I AM MORE wealthy.

Day 94

If I don't have anyone, I have myself. I am here for myself. I'm with myself 24/7. I am my own best friend. I AM MORE self-reliant.

Day 95

I like quality people, places and things. Everything has to be refined and excellent. I am fabulous. I AM MORE superior.

Day 96

I am comfortable and at great ease. I am pleased and pleasured. I AM MORE luxurious.

Day 97

Every day I grow abundantly. I am exuberant. I am rich in every part of my existence. I AM MORE bountiful.

Day 98

I am clean with a good hygiene. My aroma is pleasing. I AM MORE magnetic.

Day 99

I am able to share myself. I am able to provide for many. I am able to share progress. I can be in more places than one. I help others feel comfortable in my presence. I AM MORE flexible.

Day 100

I have worked hard. I like who I am becoming. I am changing and forming into a better version of myself. I am progressing. I AM MORE pleased.

Day 101

I am fierce! I have a strong personality with a great vibe. My attitude is confident and assertive but not mean. I AM MORE sassy.

Day 102

I am not easy to figure out; I am unpredictable. I have depth. I AM MORE interesting.

Day 103

I like to share my opinion on certain topics. I am a person that expresses my feelings. I AM MORE vocal.

Day 104

Sometimes, I like to observe when I get around random people. I don't often get comfortable too quickly. I pay attention to my surroundings. I AM MORE cautious.

Day 105

I am energetic. I am assertive, not mean. I have different ways of getting what I want. I move forward with great momentum. I AM MORE dynamic.

Day 106

I am not a part of drama. I have no conflict to my name. I am not a victim of circumstance. I AM MORE innocent.

Day 107

My hopes are high. My imagination is big. I can see myself wealthy in the future. I believe that I am created for a great purpose. I AM MORE of a dream-maker.

Day 108

I like to take charge. I influence people to follow me. I will follow the right people to enhance my leadership skills. I work well alone and with others. I AM MORE paramount.

Day 109

I will accept constructive criticism. I am sensitive to the feelings of others and I empathize to help gain a greater understanding of their situation. I AM MORE sensitive.

Day 110

I am popular. I am attractive. I am like magic. I make things happen. I AM MORE glamorous.

Day 111

I have my life planned out. My path is drawn in my mind and on paper. I am the only one responsible for the blueprint. I AM MORE established.

Day 112

Many depend on me. I am needed. I am necessary. I AM MORE essential.

Day 113

I am on time and here when needed. I don't let people down. I do as I said or planned. I AM MORE reliable.

Day 114

I give straight answers. I let others know exactly what I mean. My clarity is crystal clear when I verbally and non-verbally communicate. I AM MORE direct.

Day 115

I care about my peers and environment. I help out in my community. I like to take care of my surroundings. I AM MORE environmental.

Day 116

I am outstanding. I am joyous. I bring happiness to others. I AM MORE gregarious.

Day 117

My personality is unique. My thoughts and words help others. I AM MORE efficacious.

Day 118

I laugh a lot. My goal is to make others feel happy-jitters. I AM MORE silly.

Day 119

I am a cheery person. I pep-up others and I am happy when everyone succeeds. I AM MORE encouraging.

Day 120

I am worthy—worthy to be shown off, worthy to be taken seriously. My being is worth more than rubies, diamonds and any amount of money. I AM MORE treasured.

Day 121

I am valorous. I am a stand up person. I am marked with courage and bravery. I have more heart.

Day 122

God's house is my house. I am always welcome. God is my saving grace. I love the Lord. I AM MORE pious.

Day 123

Many listen to me. Something about my personality allows others to look up to me. I AM MORE imperative.

Day 124

I am respectful. I am polite. I AM MORE civil.

Day 125

I let my love be noticed; I do not hide it. All my feelings are shown. I AM MORE blatant.

Day 126

I don't spend much time on decisions. I think fast. I come to conclusions fast. I settle in a final way. I AM MORE decisive.

Day 127

I am protected and defended from evil. Angels encompass all around me, therefore I am not afraid. My heart is shielded from the elms of life and my mind is set on living victoriously. I AM MORE Preserved.

Day 128

I want my business ideas to expand. Money growth is inevitable, I want my finances to multiply; therefore monetary increase is in consistent flow. Possessing Multiple streams of income is my primary goal. I AM MORE Financially Stable.

Day 129

I am original. I am able to think on my own and come up with bright, unique ideas. I AM MORE inventive.

Day 130

I am a good person with morals. Being honest is part of my personality. I have more integrity.

Day 131

My eyes are open to all. Everyone will get the same treatment, no matter what age, gender or class they are in. I AM MORE fair.

Day 132

My motivation keeps me up on my feet every day. I do what I have to do. I cannot and will not fail because I AM MORE determined.

Day 133

My future is determined by me. I have to shape myself into a scholarly figure and pursue my dreams. I AM MORE studious.

Day 134

The good information I receive sticks in my mind. I remember everything positive that is told to me and feed off of that knowledge. I AM MORE absorbent.

Day 135

I am an optimist. The positive is always on my mind. Negativity is my worst enemy. I think of the greater outcomes even when I'm in tough situations. I AM MORE conscientious.

Day 136

I am me, finer as the time passes. I'm beautiful/handsome in every way. I AM MORE regal.

Day 137

I am a giving person. I offer things to people before they ask and I am thoughtful of others. I AM MORE unselfish.

Day 138

I keep my body healthy and in forward movement. I have very few breaks throughout my day. I AM MORE active.

Day 139

I get enough sleep every day to keep me up and wired. I eat properly to make sure I don't lack in my priorities. I AM MORE replenished.

Day 140

Holding grudges is not good for my health. I forgive but don't forget. I let go of problems so they won't dictate my life. I AM MORE forgiving.

Day 141

I do what I am told. I push myself to work harder and be better. I AM MORE disciplined.

Day 142

I do not beat around the bush when it comes to situations or problems. I speak for myself with words and deeds. I think before I speak and I get straight to the point. I AM MORE resolute.

Day 143

Work is always done on time. I get straight to my orders when they are given. Making decisions before deadlines are important to me. I AM MORE proactive.

Day 144

I avoid generalization. I take criticism well. I stand my ground when it comes to stereotypes and I do not judge. I AM MORE unassuming.

Day 145

I believe that the universe will yield to me every positive desire that's with-in me. Today, I choose to be a deliberate creator of more of the things that I want. I will treat my life and the lives around me with respect and value all that I have. I AM MORE of a receiver of all that is good.

Day 146

I lift up spirits. I am very kind to others that are hurt, and I am sure to be aware of their feelings. I AM MORE gracious.

Day 147

I am very outgoing. People are wowed by my style. I like to be bright. I AM MORE dazzling.

Day 148

"Money is the ruler of the world" is the opinion of the majority of this world. Every day, I work hard to make money. Every day I get closer to being wealthier. I AM MORE lucrative.

Day 149

My attitude is bright and lively. I show signs of optimism and healthy actions in every area of life. I am conscious of being balanced. I AM MORE holistic.

Day 150

The future excites me. The future brings the thought of a more advanced world. I AM MORE futuristic.

Day 151

I have class. I like to speak with etiquette and good demeanor. I am also an individual that's separate from the chaos and trends of this world. Good manners add to my well-being. I AM MORE elegant.

Day 152

My words are smooth and my actions are swift. Many people find me irresistible because of my great charm. I AM MORE persuasive.

Day 153

Wildlife matters; I respect their lives. I believe that they should be treated fairly and not abused. I AM MORE ecological.

Day 154

I am interested in the study of the life of human beings. Where did I come from? What am I? I AM MORE ethnological.

Day 155

I feel wonderful. Every part of me vibrates vitality, strength and stamina. Health is apart of my wealth. I want to leave a legacy for generations to come. I AM MORE Alive.

Day 156

I am gentle. I would say that people see my presence as "light as a feather" because I do not have many problems on my shoulders. I choose not to stress. I AM MORE heavenly.

Day 157

I treat myself and others with respect so people will know how to treat me. I share my weaknesses so that others will know that I am imperfect, too. I AM MORE vulnerable.

Day 158

My secrets are only kept with me. I do not share my personal information with everyone. Others' secrets are also safe with me. I AM MORE esoteric.

Day 159

I am a well-educated individual. I am elevated. I am working toward achieving my goals. I AM MORE scholastic.

Day 160

I am a wonderful work of art, yet I am fragile. Passionate and keen with a whole lot of love. These are my most treasured characteristics. I AM MORE enthusiastic.

Day 161

The glorious acts I perform are often remembered. I am known for my outstanding differences. I AM MORE red-letter.

Day 162

When times are dull, I decide to add some flavor. I tell jokes and do silly things to make people laugh. I AM MORE humorous.

Day 163

I am a sharing person. Charity is the world's greatest gift. I love to see others happy. I AM MORE giving.

Day 164

I notice my surroundings. Little things catch my attention. Nothing gets by me without notice. My safety is most important. I AM MORE aware.

Day 165

I am very thankful for what I have. I always use my 'please' and 'thank yous.' I have gratitude. I AM MORE appreciative.

Day 166

It's healthy to think about the day you have had, how it went and how to improve the next day. I AM MORE reflective.

Day 167

I've learned that everything that is said or done doesn't need a reaction. I AM MORE mature.

Day 168

I'm fine with a lot of things. I don't stress or complain often. I AM MORE laid-back.

Day 169

Sometimes I tend to put others before myself. If I know someone is in greater need more than I, I will give up certain things to help them. I AM MORE self-sacrificing.

Day 170

I ask a lot of questions about little things. I am very curious. I just want to know full details. I AM MORE inquisitive.

Day 171

My country goes through a lot, but at the end of the day I have much love for it. I AM MORE patriotic.

Day 172

I can do a lot and perform many tasks. I am very gifted and have multiple talents. I AM MORE skillful.

Day 173

I may be youthful or even short of gray hairs, but I can say that I have learned a lot as long as I've been on this earth. I AM MORE wise.

Day 174

My actions create sparks! I am an outgoing person that can move quickly. I AM MORE enterprising.

Day 175

Instead of always going with the first thing on my mind, I listen to others and try to see their point of view. I AM MORE understanding.

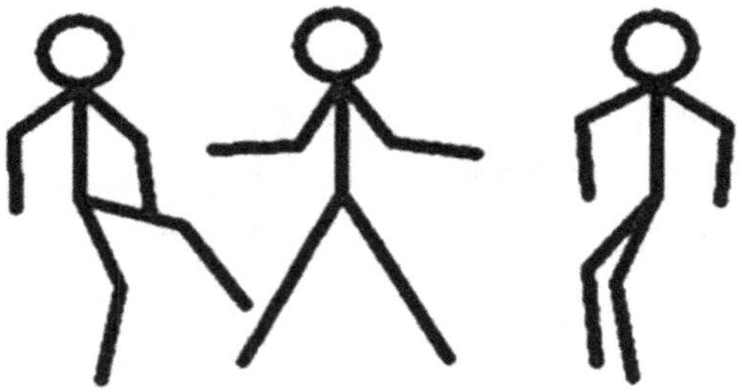

Day 176

I am a person that is organized. I focus better without clutter. Everything I do is in a consecutive and synchronized manner. I AM MORE orderly.

Day 177

My looks are one aspect of me, but they are not the primary definition of who I am. I express my character through all of my being. My attitude is fierce yet gentle when needed. I AM MORE well-rounded.

Day 178

Many people anticipate my presence. I am a popular person and fortunate to have great family and friends. I AM MORE desirable.

Day 179

I am a friendly person. Sometimes I like to have a little fun and engage in playful conversations. I AM MORE flirtatious.

Day 180

I am intricately and creatively designed. The Creator exceeded my expectations with His rare invention of me. I AM MORE extravagant.

Day 181

I am not frightened by much because I am almost fearless. I take risks and they are exciting to me. I AM MORE daring.

Day 182

I am very well. I wake up with a smile on my face. I am thankful to be on this earth. Every day I AM MORE copacetic.

Day 183

I like to buy items but I will use what I have around me to save more. I am frugal with money and certain things. I use all of my assets to put myself and others in the best position. I AM MORE resourceful.

Day 184

I am an exciting person that never has a dull moment. I tend to keep the spirit alive. I AM MORE jovial.

Day 185

I am pleasing to many people because of my soft and sweet vibe. It's not in my heart to be rude or mean. I AM MORE mellow.

Day 186

I am easygoing. I am also a cool person. I don't often say 'no.' I AM MORE accommodating.

Day 187

I am strong and can overcome anything. After I go through a problem or even an illness, I go back to my natural state of mind and maybe even better than before. I AM MORE resilient.

Day 188

I am gentle and very careful. I take and handle situations with precautions. I AM MORE thorough.

Day 189

I cannot let a problem go on without knowing the information. I have to be updated 24/7. I like helping with questions and concerns. I AM MORE involved.

Day 190

I am like a vibrant light; my energy fuels everything that I touch. Happiness becomes me and love emanates from me. I AM MORE radiant.

Day 191

Even though it might take me a little time to adapt to different environments, I've learned how to behave and survive in all situations. I AM MORE adaptable.

Day 192

I have a powerful mind and a strong contour. I am in shape. I believe I can do anything. I AM MORE fit.

Day 193

Every day I get wiser and better. I grow and progress continually. I am steady. I am maturing. I AM MORE on the increase.

Day 194

I am rich in quality. I am abounding. I am working toward being very wealthy. I AM MORE affluent.

Day 195

I am soft. I have feelings. I am fragile. I AM MORE lighthearted.

Day 196

My kindness passes on to others. I have a big heart that causes me to show much care for others and to be very unselfish in times of need. I AM MORE good-willed.

Day 197

I have natural talents that I improve every day. I work on my personal being. I AM MORE personally developed.

Day 198

I am on time. I am clear with my words. I am straightforward. I AM MORE exact.

Day 199

I stand out. I am amazing in the things I do. I AM MORE beaming.

Day 200

My heart is filled with lots of love. I have love for everyone. I AM MORE abundant.

Day 201

The things I receive are not free. I could be in a worse position but I'm not. I am blessed. I AM MORE fortunate.

Day 202

I have no problems that will send me into depression. I tell myself every day: "better days are to come." Therefore, I stay alert with great expectations and joy. I AM MORE blissful.

Day 203

I am lighthearted. My happiness is contagious; it travels. I AM MORE infectious.

Day 204

I am a giving person. I don't often hesitate to do a good deed. I AM MORE bountiful.

Day 205

I commit to things that are important to me. Loyalty is a quality that I take to heart. I am dedicated to people, places and things that I am passionate about. I AM MORE steadfast.

Day 206

I am confident in my skin. I love myself. I AM MORE secure.

Day 207

I was created to share my gifts and talents. The knowledge that I have can be given to other people in hopes of making their lives more plentiful. I AM MORE copious.

Day 208

The events that happen in my life are exciting. I am ready to progress in life. My adrenaline is pumping! I AM MORE eager.

Day 209

When I am doing work or trying to reach a goal I am very motivated. I make it so that no one gets in my way. I AM MORE intense.

Day 210

I am a resourceful person who likes to save. I reduce, reuse and recycle to keep a healthy environment. I AM MORE economical.

Day 211

I may get overjoyed and my heart may begin to race because of all the excitement. I AM MORE ecstatic.

Day 212

I give off the exact amount of energy toward people. I do not overdo certain things. I AM MORE efficient.

Day 213

When it comes to work, I do more than is expected. I want to learn more and be ahead. I am an overachiever and love to work in excellence. I AM MORE of a high-flier.

Day 214

My personality is bright. I'm like an organic remedy. Others love my presence because of my positive energy and electrifying attitude. I AM MORE effervescent.

Day 215

I have glory! I am thankful for everything. I AM MORE exultant.

Day 216

I am healthy. I work out. I am in shape. I AM MORE athletic.

Day 217

Every day I wake up with a new start. I give myself another chance to get 'it' right. I AM MORE fresh.

Day 218

Each time I recover from a downfall, I can say I'm good because I replenish myself and try again. I AM MORE solid.

Day 219

Genuine fulfillment means depending on myself to inspire happiness within me. I am responsible for giving joy, peace and positive thoughts permission to reign in my life on a daily basis. I seek to have more Authentic Happiness.

Day 220

I give loving energy to others and make them feel special. I AM MORE hearty.

Day 221

I deserve much recognition for my hard work and great attitude, even if it's a pat on my own back. I am very accomplished. I AM MORE honorable.

Day 222

I give credit when and to whom it's due. I AM MORE rewarding.

Day 223

I am rejuvenated and anchored. I have balance in all areas of my life. I AM MORE stable.

Day 224

People come to me for advice. I help others feel better with an occasional hug or kiss. I AM MORE nurturing.

Day 225

I am new and improved every day. I AM MORE replenished.

Day 226

I am like the summer; a breath of fresh air, enjoyable. I AM MORE bright.

Day 227

Everything about me is significant and worth remembering. I AM MORE cherished.

Day 228

I am a person of my word. I am mature. I am very understanding. I AM MORE developed.

Day 229

I am in tune with myself every day and proud of who I am becoming. I notice that I feel more attractive every step of the way. I AM MORE aware.

Day 230

I am peculiar, and my spirit gives off a great feeling. My uniqueness is unparalleled. I AM MORE distinctive.

Day 231

I am lively. I am a person that is more motivated every day. I AM MORE progressive.

Day 232

My thoughts and answers are finalized. I am confident in what I say. I AM MORE certain.

Day 233

I reflect in silence, and meditation keeps me resilient. Prayer to the creator is a must, especially for guidance through all the gloom and dust. I am practicing the art of letting go and letting God; yes, releasing all of my burdens. I am implementing the art of being more Still.

Day 234

I am healthy, happy and loved. Everything that I touch, endeavor and/or desire that's aligned with what's best for me, prospers. I consider the welfare of others including myself. I AM MORE in tuned with the art of Well-Being.

Day 235

Helping others is what life is all about, it gives me a sense of purpose to make someone else's world a little brighter. I'm realizing acts of service are the friendliest gesture and they serve my best interest as well. I enjoy being more Accommodating.

Day 236

Everything I do has an ending. I make sure to finish whatever I start. I am definitive. I AM MORE conclusive.

Day 237

I am quiet about my progress. I don't tell everyone about the moves I make and how far I have gotten. I only share when my work is crystallized. I AM MORE concealed.

Day 238

I am able to express myself thoroughly with few or no mistakes. I AM MORE well-spoken.

Day 239

My brainpower is evident. My peers, friends and family members notice and give me compliments. I AM MORE intellectual.

Day 240

I tend to ask many questions, no matter what the conversation entails, for more understanding. I also ask in different ways just for accuracy. I AM MORE of a conversationalist.

Day 241

Because of the aura I give off, people tend to attach themselves to me. When I am approached, I react with a welcoming attitude. I AM MORE approachable.

Day 242

I'm responsible for myself. I do my best to depend on others lightly because the job, most of the time, gets done more quickly and thoroughly when I do it myself. I am independent. I AM MORE self-reliant.

Day 243

I capture others' attention because of my exclusive personality and great looks. I AM MORE mesmerizing.

Day 244

I am attractive. I carry myself with class. I also have expensive tastes and style. I AM MORE resplendent.

Day 245

I am valuable and will only accept the best quality of people, places and things. I take care of myself. I have luxurious tastes. I AM MORE sumptuous.

Day 246

I switch up my style. I have many different looks. I adapt to different environments very quickly. I AM MORE versatile.

Day 247

The aura I give off is very attractive and sexy. I am courageous and determined. I AM MORE spunky.

Day 248

When others tell me their problems, I listen to their side to try to see where they are coming from. I AM MORE insightful.

Day 249

I am a very kind person that cares and loves everyone around me, even my enemies. I AM MORE devoted.

Day 250

I am different from others. I am a very outgoing person with an extravagant personality. I AM MORE fascinating.

Day 251

I care for other's feelings. I am there when they need me to have a shoulder to cry on. I AM MORE compassionate.

Day 252

The love I give, such as advice and concern for others including myself, never runs out. I AM MORE unlimited.

Day 253

I push others to work harder. I give energy and hope to others and myself. I AM MORE invigorating.

Day 254

The more well traveled I am, the more knowledgeable I become. I AM MORE expansive.

Day 255

I have much joy and happiness in me that can't be taken away. I AM MORE pulsating.

Day 256

I emanate great joy and love. I AM MORE beamy.

Day 257

I am lively and animated. Others are attracted to me because of these characteristics. I AM MORE vivacious.

Day 258

I am always finding ways to reinvent myself. I was distracted, but I reestablished myself. I AM MORE renewed.

Day 259

I want a love that flows easy and safe. My life partner will come to me with ease and I will know that he/she is the one. We will love each other completely and live happily ever after. I AM MORE of a Life Partner.

Day 260

I have a welcoming smile that awaits people when I meet them. My hugs and kisses are genuine. I AM MORE warm.

Day 261

I'm always ahead of the game. I get things done quicker. I AM MORE advanced.

Day 262

I accept encouragement, especially when it's genuine. Life is more interesting when I dream and work to achieve the vision I don't yet see. I AM MORE believing.

Day 263

The deeds I offer cause me to receive more of the good things. I benefit from the little things that I do for others, including myself. I am beneficial.

Day 264

I am a free person. I do whatever I want under the rules I follow. I am able to explore. I AM MORE circulating.

Day 265

Once I start something, I do not stop until the job is done. I AM MORE consistent.

Day 266

Even after I am gone, I will always be remembered by others. I AM MORE eternal.

Day 267

I am a great achiever. My accomplishments are meaningful and complete. I AM MORE excellent.

Day 268

I have knowledge that expands every day. I AM MORE of a genius.

Day 269

I have many talents that are useful in many ways. I AM MORE gifted.

Day 270

My clothing is well put together. I have a sumptuous look about myself. I AM MORE lavish.

Day 271

My name has positive things behind it. I am very special with a good reputation. I AM MORE massive.

Day 272

When I hurt someone, I make a point to apologize. I AM MORE merciful.

Day 273

I tell my family everything so they will not be in the dark. I have nothing to hide. I AM MORE open.

Day 274

Others look up to me because I'm a good person. I AM MORE praised.

Day 275

I am worth a lot and should be treated as such. I value and respect others including myself. It's important to me to put my best foot forward. I AM MORE quality.

Day 276

I try to compromise with others to come up with a solution that's acceptable for everyone. I AM MORE reasonable.

Day 277

I am fast. I am on time. I am quick. I AM MORE on point.

Day 278

I accept everyone. Everyone deserves a chance in life. I AM MORE because I see the good in others.

Day 279

I listen to my elders. I only say and do what will build others, including myself. I AM MORE respectful.

Day 280

I am figuring out who I am. I am happy with who I am. I AM MORE resolved.

Day 281

I am a quiet person. People may find me mysterious. I AM MORE composed.

Day 282

I am peaceful. I like to meditate and have time to myself. I AM MORE tranquil.

Day 283

I'd rather spend a day with myself than a group, because I like to enjoy the quiet moments alone. I AM MORE placid.

Day 284

I move quickly, but I get a lot done. No one witnesses the hard work I put in, but they notice the results. I AM MORE invisible.

Day 285

My work and priorities are finished on time. I move and progress faster than most people. I AM MORE instantaneous.

Day 286

I can do anything I set my sail to. Anything and everything I desire out of life is possible. I AM MORE able.

Day 287

I have beautiful features that keep my confidence high. I AM MORE pretty/handsome.

Day 288

I like to be high quality, but I do not judge others and the choices they make in life. I AM MORE non-judgmental.

Day 289

Every time I do something, I think ahead of time. I think before I speak. I AM MORE premeditated.

Day 290

I like to stay close to others, not too far away because I want to be there for everyone. I think families and friends should stick together. I AM MORE together.

Day 291

I love my family and I love spending time with them. Family is all I have; therefore, they are my best friends. I AM MORE family-oriented.

Day 292

I have had a lot of help in my life to get to where I am now. I AM MORE guided.

Day 293

When I go to the house of my God (church, mosque, etc), I feel the spirit and when I leave, I leave feeling cleansed. I AM MORE touched by God.

Day 294

I listen to all types of people—different accents and languages. I am not rude and do not stop listening. I stay and try to understand people. I AM MORE comprehensive.

Day 295

I take pride in all that I do. I try my hardest to make myself more proud each day, to prove to myself that I can do it. I AM MORE self-trained.

Day 296

I find everyone equal with equal rights no matter what. Different people act in different ways. I AM MORE political.

Day 297

I am a super friendly person with an inspiring personality. I love to share encouragement, advice and just good ol' speech. I AM MORE peachy.

Day 298

I help others in tough situations. Others can call on me for anything. Saving the lost is everything to me. I am reliable. I AM MORE heroic.

Day 299

I have a fortified desire to achieve all of my goals. I push forward with resilience and strength. I AM MORE ambitious.

Day 300

I have a pleasing personality. I welcome others warmly. I AM MORE amiable.

Day 301

No matter what situation I am put in, I am always pally. I AM MORE amicable.

Day 302

I am exhilarating. Others enjoy my presence because I am entertaining. I AM MORE amusing.

Day 303

I am open to many decisions and not easily offended. I AM MORE broad-minded.

Day 304

I am likable. I show others attention and I make great conversation. I AM MORE convivial.

Day 305

I use my manners and I am overly nice. I AM MORE courteous.

Day 306

I can manage big business. I am a leader. I AM MORE diplomatic.

Day 307

No matter what race or religion someone is, we are all human. I AM MORE fair-minded.

Day 308

I like good, long conversation. I like to communicate with others. I AM MORE gregarious.

Day 309

I treat everyone with respect and care. I AM MORE impartial.

Day 310

I don't take too much pride in all of my work, because I know that everything I do could be done better. Nothing is perfect; work to perfection. I AM MORE modest.

Day 311

I don't show too much emotion when I am let down or even surprised in a good manner. I am calm. I AM MORE philosophical.

Day 312

New ideas come to my mind often. I am innovative. I AM MORE pioneering.

Day 313

I show bravery no matter how difficult the situation is. I am pluckier.

Day 314

I am understanding and logical when it comes to making decisions. I AM MORE rational.

Day 315

Sugar-coating is not my thing, so it's important that I say what I mean and mean what I say. Being level-headed in speech is key. I AM MORE sensible.

Day 316

I am organized and clean. I AM MORE tidy.

Day 317

I am not easily broken. I AM MORE tough.

Day 318

I do not make statements unless I know they are true. I AM MORE unassuming.

Day 319

I am glad to help others. I AM MORE willing.

Day 320

Many people approve of me a great deal. I am well-liked. I am flattering. I AM MORE favorable.

Day 321

Good deeds are more enjoyed when they are done spontaneously. Those deeds hit others by surprise and that's when my soul lights up. I AM MORE fortuitous.

Day 322

I am too vivid to be described in words. I AM MORE ineffable.

Day 323

I am pleasing to others. I AM MORE mirthful.

Day 324

I am so beautiful/handsome in a dramatic way! I AM MORE spectacular.

Day 325

I wow others. I am amazing. I AM MORE splendid.

Day 326

I am a star! I feel famous. I AM MORE stellar.

Day 327

I am a delight and like being the center of attention; however it brings me great enjoyment to edify other people. I AM MORE stupendous.

Day 328

I am a joy to be around. I AM MORE wondrous.

Day 329

I am counted on for many things. Other people look up to me. I tell my friends the truth and those who welcome my advice. I also accept constructive criticism. I AM MORE accountable.

Day 330

When others are added to my dwelling or environment, I am very welcoming. I AM MORE hospitable.

Day 331

I am able to get along with others very well. I AM MORE accordant.

Day 332

I get better each day. Others notice my progress and admire me. I AM MORE becoming.

Day 333

My demeanor is very classy/classic. I AM MORE of a bijou.

Day 334

I can be overprotective about the people I care about. I AM MORE brotherly/sisterly.

Day 335

I have a lot of energy, and I am full of excitement! I AM MORE boisterous.

Day 336

I do my best to be clear, efficient and concise when having formal conversations. This helps everyone involved achieve productivity. I AM MORE brief.

Day 337

I am a problem solver, and I allow others to speak their mind and express their feelings toward each other. I AM MORE of a mediator.

Day 338

I have a calm personality. I am pleasant. Organic is my flow. I AM MORE breezy.

Day 339

I am working toward success. I am active. I AM MORE promising.

Day 340

I am speedy. I am quick. I move in an urgent way. I AM MORE brisk.

Day 341

I am very spirited. I can be very friendly and share with others. I serve others out of passion and habit. I AM MORE altruistic.

Day 342

I am accumulative, meaning that I am growing in success. This never stops. I AM MORE amassed.

Day 343

I am a risk taker. I am daring. Tough situations don't scare me. I AM MORE dauntless.

Day 344

I am confident in what I do and do things that are out of the box. I surprise myself. I AM MORE mettlesome.

Day 345

My courage is very noticeable. This is life, so why not live it! I AM MORE indomitable.

Day 346

I catch other's attention and I keep it! I am interesting. I enjoy getting lost in beauty and brains. I AM MORE enthralled.

Day 347

I welcome others. They get to know me, but they don't know too much. I keep others wondering and enchanted. I AM MORE captivating.

Day 348

I am knowledgeable and have morals. I AM MORE ethical.

Day 349

I am fascinating and attention-catching. I AM MORE riveting.

Day 350

I like being creative and working with my mind and hands. I am active and I keep things interesting. I AM MORE eventful.

Day 351

My scholarly traits allow me to be a role model for others. I AM MORE exemplary.

Day 352

Others put me on a high pedestal because of the great acts of service I have bestowed on others. I AM MORE ennobling.

Day 353

I am able to bring others happiness. I AM MORE enrapturing.

Day 354

I grow in my failures as well as my successes. Life stretches me even when I'm not ready, and still I accept the changes. I AM MORE emerging.

Day 355

No one is perfect, but every day we try our hardest to get the closest to it. I AM MORE faultless.

Day 356

I please others by bringing joy to them. I AM MORE appreciated.

Day 357

I am brave with almost no fears. I AM MORE gallant.

Day 358

As much as I am aware of my surroundings, I should know everything that goes on around me. I AM MORE heedful.

Day 359

I always care for others. Other people's feelings are meaningful to me. I AM MORE humane.

Day 360

My style is creative. I am fashionable. I AM MORE groovy.

Day 361

I have a great foundation no matter where I come from. I will keep the good faith. Every day, I'll show the world, including myself, how upstanding I am by behaving correctly. I AM MORE grounded.

Day 362

I do my best to support others and be a sympathetic person. I AM MORE helpful.

Day 363

I am always updated. Even though I am updated, I try not to be like everyone else and have my own style. I AM MORE hip.

Day 364

I often switch up my styles and others follow. I AM MORE trendy.

Day 365

I am well-rounded. My good traits can be overwhelming, and I can share them with others. I AM MORE ginormous.

CPSIA information can be obtained
at www.ICGtesting.com
Printed in the USA
LVHW021301030621
689198LV00011B/716